A·FIRST·BOOK·FOR
BEDTIME

A·FIRST·BOOK·FOR
BEDTIME

Illustrated by David Anstey
Written by A J Wood

MODERN PUBLISHING
A Division of Unisystems, Inc.
New York, New York 10022

Once
upon a time,
a dinosaur
dreamed...

He dreamed he was a bird,
flying in the sky.

The bird flew and flew
until he came to a field
full of yellow flowers...

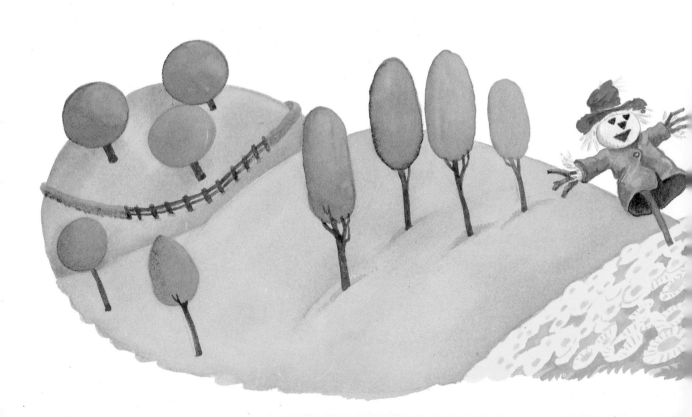

Then he dreamed he was a
flower waving in the wind.

The wind whisked him away,
and he floated to the sea...

He dreamed he was a fish,
swimming beneath the waves.

The fish swam and swam
until winter came...

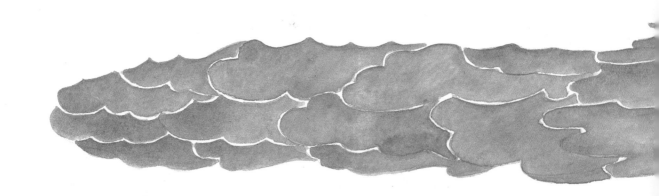

Then he dreamed
he was a snowman,
with a carrot for his nose.

The snowman
shivered in the cold
until the sun came out...

Then he dreamed he was a butterfly, flying in the sun.

He fluttered over fields and meadows...

Until it was night,
and darkness fell...

Then he dreamed
he was a dinosaur
tucked in bed.

And the dinosaur dreamed...